The Brilliant Brain Friends

A Mind Tools For Kids Tale
For Lexie and Nancy

Hi I'm Emily, welcome to the world of Mind Tools For Kids! Here you will meet Brilliant Brain and his friends Milo, Lenny and Orla. The Brain Friends are a fun way to help children understand how they experience feelings in their mind and body. By learning about the relationship between their body's reactions, feelings and thought process, kids can start to make sense of their big emotions!

To find out more about Mind Tools For Kids products, Coach Training and workshops visit www.mindtoolsforkids.com

London, UK 2020

Hi, my name is Brilliant Brain.
Your brain is brilliant too!
It does some pretty incredible things
To help you live as you!

Here is the story of my clever thinking tree,
and the three amazing brain friends that are a part of me.

They live up there inside my head,
they keep me safe and sound.

From thinking, feeling, breathing air
and moving all around.

Meet Orla, Milo and Lenny!

They help me feel my happy thoughts
  and even wobbles too.

They work together joyfully,
they know just what to do.

From my thinking, to my feeling, to eating yummy food.
And the funny times I giggle
and when I'm in a mood.

My friends are there through everything
from sadness and to glory.

I know you'll love my brain friends too,
so let me tell their story...

Thinking Tree

We live in a tree that thinks and feels.
It runs the body too.

With lovely firm roots and a super-strong trunk,
It reminds me a little of you.

Its branches flex as they wave in the wind.
Its leaves change every season.

I live here at the top, on a branch up high,
My love of the sky is the reason.

Up here I can see,
I can ponder and think.
I'm inspired by learning
and growing.

I explain to my friends,
and I help them make sense.
I'm an owl with a
passion for knowing.

Orla loves to...

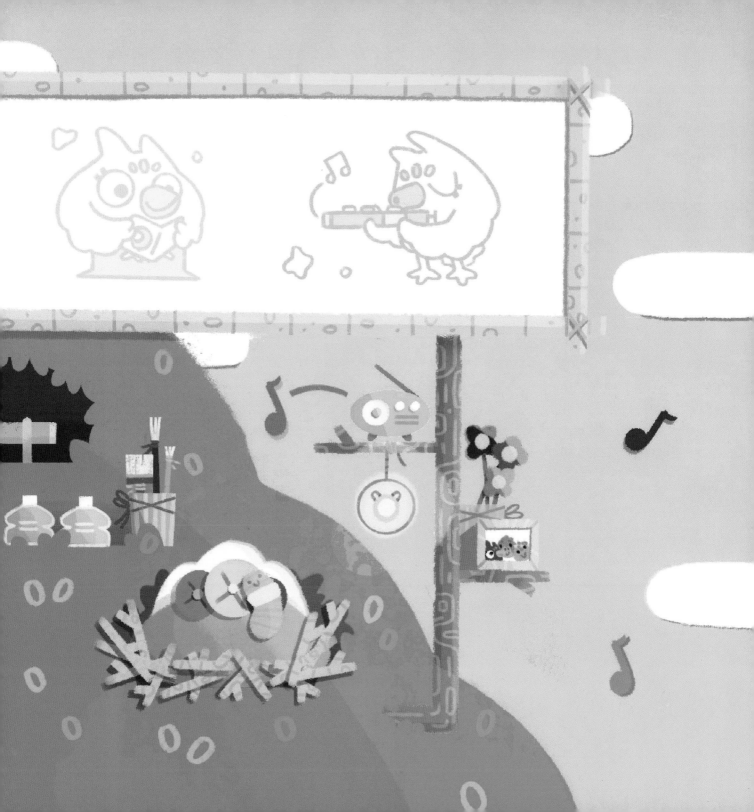

Down in the trunk my two friends stay.
They are silly and fun and loud.

They help me wind down. We love to play,
our friendship makes me proud.

Down in
the trunk!

I live down below,
amongst the tall grasses.
I run, jump and stretch
in the dirt.

I sometimes get scared
when the puppy dog passes.
I'm a lizard that's always alert.

Lenny loves to...

Hi my name's Milo
and this is my den.
It's the cosy and
comfortable part.

I enjoy being kind,
I'm a lovable friend.
I'm a monkey with
a very big heart.

Milo loves to...

My lizard friend Lenny, he often gets scared.
So we look up to Orla, she's always prepared.

I shout, and I screech, and she flutters away.
And Lenny he worries, I don't know what to say.

Because sometimes my feelings grow bigger and bubble,
And Lenny runs off as he feels he's in trouble.

And Orla can't think
amongst all of the noise.
And we all lose our way,
and the calm is destroyed.

It happens so quickly
and how we don't know,
fighting and flighting
and freezing we go.

At times Lenny's tired
and just needs a drink.

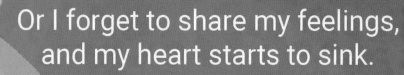

Or I forget to share my feelings,
and my heart starts to sink.

We think we're in danger.
We begin to scream and cry.
Orla wants to help us,
but she needs some calm to try

But then Lenny quietens,
and breathes slow and deep,
as his body relaxes
the ground hugs his feet.

A cool glass of water
and a moment to stop,
all the tensions start shifting,
his shoulders then drop.

His body is calmer;
He feels more aware.
He comes up to see me
and asks me to share.

And then I feel safer and happy to talk,
we sit for a moment or go for a walk.

Out come my feelings, and I open my heart.
It's from being so peaceful the learning can start.
Down then comes Orla all-knowing and wise,
she helps us think clearly and open our eyes.

It's perfectly normal to feel worried or sad,
it doesn't erase all the good times you've had.

Just pause for a moment and listen to me,
I watch from the rooftops, no danger I see.

It doesn't mean trouble is coming your way,
it's just sometimes your feelings, they linger and stay.

So stop and consider and notice your bodies,
take care of yourself and practise some hobbies.

Care for your heart and honour your feelings,
share them and tame them and give them some meaning.
I'll always be there to help you to learn;
a guide and a teacher, somewhere to turn.

We work well together, all safe in our tree
Best friends forever, a brilliant three.

Tend and tame your Lenny
- Water and a healthy snack
- Rhythm and movement
- A nap or a meditation
- Playing and exercise
- Getting into nature
- A brain break
- Deep breaths

Tend and tame your Milo
- Talking through feelings
- Discussing memories
- A hug or physical comfort
- Sensory experience
- Connecting with someone trusted
- Sharing and expressing feelings

Tend and tame your Orla
- Reading and writing down thoughts
- Making sense of what is happening
- Talking to a trusted adult or friend
- Learning and understanding
- Mindfulness and meditation
- Role play and practising
- Art and creativity

Come and learn more about Mind Tools For Kids. To download your very own Brilliant Brain Friends Feelings Poster go to www.mindtoolsforkids.com/poster

Printed in Great Britain
by Amazon